CHRISTOPHER MENDEZ
INCORPORATING CRADDOCK & BARNARD

JACQUES CALLOT
Nancy 1592-1635

EXHIBITION
24th November - 18th December 1992

58 JERMYN STREET, LONDON SW1Y 6LP

JACQUES CALLOT
Nancy 1592-1635

three

PROVENANCE

All the etchings described in this catalogue have recently been removed from a folio album lettered on the spine Oeuvres de Callot. The album contained no ownership marks but the binding dates from the middle of the 17th century. This date is supported by the fact that all the prints are fine lifetime impressions, many in early states (noted here by Lieure's classification **R. - R.R.R.R.**).

CONDITION

As usual with these old albums, most of the smaller prints were cut close to the platemark or borderline and pasted on to the album leaves, several to a page. Only a few have margins and these are noted where applicable.

The larger prints were folded and bound directly into the album. These still show their fold marks, although they are now presented unfolded. Some of these larger plates have minor damages and stains which are described in the individual catalogue entries.

WATERMARKS

The watermarks on lifetime impressions of Callot etchings tend to fall into several family groups, listed by Lieure and expanded in the National Gallery of Art Exhibition Catalogue, 1975. Where they can be clearly matched to a recorded example we have given the Lieure number. The lack of such a number does not imply a later printing, but simply our failure to make a positive identification. Of course many of the small prints do not show a watermark at all.

REFERENCES:

Meaume, *Recherches sur la vie et les ouvrages de Jacques Callot,* Paris, MDCCCLX

Lieure, *Jacques Callot, Catalogue de l'oeuvre gravé,* Paris, 1924

NGA, *Jacques Callot Prints and related Drawings,* exhibition catalogue, National Gallery of Art, Washington, 1975

Nancy, *Jacques Callot 1592-1635,* exhibition catalogue, Musée historique lorrain, Nancy, 1992.

Meaume's monograph on Callot is the basis of all successive catalogues. Lieure re-arranged that list and his catalogue is now generally accepted as the standard list. Our catalogue is arranged in Lieure order. The most recent survey of Callot's work is the catalogue of the exhibition held in Nancy this year to commemorate the fourth centenary of his birth. Where we have an impression of a print exhibited there we have given the Nancy catalogue reference, although many of the prints we have are in different, often earlier, states than those exhibited there.

Complete set of thirty engravings. L. 16-45. Nancy (12 exhibited) 7-18.
The subjects with rounded tops trimmed to the arch.

Comprising:

L. 16,	second state of two (**R.R.R.R.**)
L. 17,	second state of three
L. 18,	first state of three
L. 19,	second state of three
L. 20,	uncertain state, trimmed to border
L. 21,	second state
L. 22,	second state of three
L. 23,	second state
L. 24,	second state
L. 25,	second state of three
L. 26,	second state
L. 27,	second state
L. 28,	second state of three
L. 29,	first state of three
L. 30,	uncertain state, trimmed to border
L. 31,	uncertain state, trimmed to border
L. 32,	second state of three
L. 33-37,	uncertain states, trimmed to borders
L. 38,	first state of two
L. 39-40,	uncertain states, trimmed to borders
L. 41,	second state of three
L. 42-45,	uncertain states, trimmed to borders

Approx. 110 x 85

Early works from Callot's Roman period, made when he was working in the studio of Philippe Thomassin, circa 1608-11. The paintings, and sculpture, were then housed in St Peter's and S. Paolo fuori le Mura.

Delineationes picturæ Alta-
rium in Ecclesijs S. Petri et
S. Pauli Romæ, à celeberrimis
huius seculi pictoribus pictæ

L. 16

I. Callot fecit   7

L. 23

L. 33

L. 43

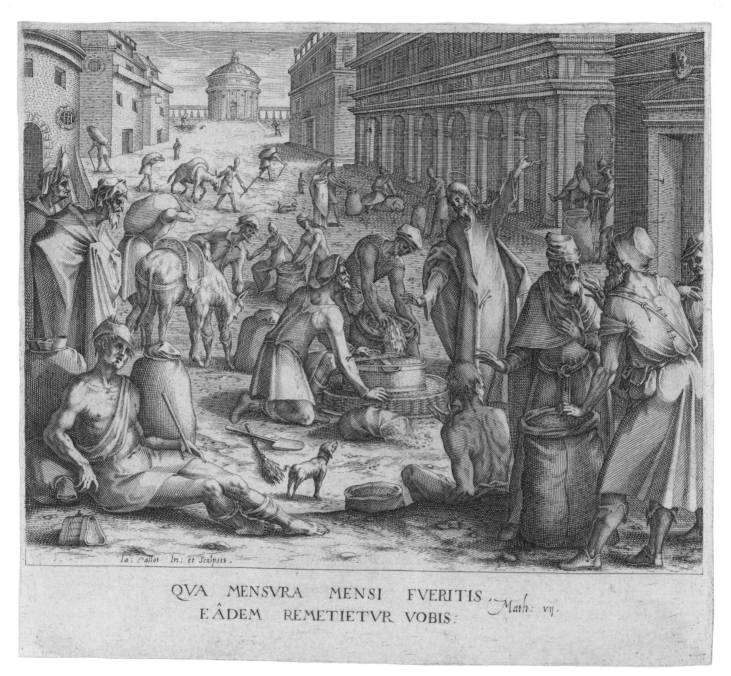

Ia: Callot In: et Sculpsit.

QVA MENSVRA MENSI FVERITIS
EÂDEM REMETIETVR VOBIS: Math: vij.

L. 50

2   **_Les Mesureurs de grains_**

Engraving, L. 50, only state (**R.**). Nancy 19.

194 x 209

An early work from Callot's Roman period, and the first to give his name as designer.

L. 72

3   *L'enfer*

Engraving after Bernardino Poccetti, 1612, dedicated to Cosimo II de Medici.
L. 72, first state of two, before the address of Rossi (**R.R.R.**).

Watermark: *Shield* on the two lower sheets.

730 x 865

Printed from four plates, this impression with large margins shows serious crease marks where it was folded in the album, some of which were split and are now reinforced. There is some water damage on the verso but for a print of this size the recto is acceptable in appearance.

4 **Le Grand Ecce Homo**

Engraving, 1613. L. 77, fourth state of five, before the address of Mariette. Nancy 24.

Watermark: *Armorial* (similar to Hornibrook & Petitjean, *Jean Morin*, No. 4).

316 x 246

5   *La possédée, ou L'exorcisme*

Engraving after Andrea Boscoli, L. 146, fifth state of six. Small tear repaired top right.

302 x 226

Although dated 1630 this engraving was made some ten years before, in Florence. The date would have been added when the plate was printed in Nancy.

L. 173

6   ***Les deux Pantalons (Zanni)***

L. 173, first state (**R.R.**), circa 1616, Nancy 125.

93 x 142

TEATRO FATTO IN FIRENZE NELLA FESTA A CAVALLO PER LA VENVTA DEL SER.ᵐᵃ PRINCIPE D'VRBINO
Qui fecero 42 Caualieri diuersi abbattimenti e dipoi un balletto ci si uide ancora una battaglia a piedi di 300 persone, oltre i Carri e l'altra gente per diuersi seruitij
Iullius Parigi Inu: C. allot delineauit et

L. 182

7   ***Piazza Santa Croce. L'entrée des chars et parade de la cavalerie et de l'infanterie***

After Giulio Parigi, L. 182, first state of two, before the address of Rossi. Nancy 90.

Watermark: *King's head* (L. 21)

224 x 294

One of the illustrations from the Guerre de Beauté, *Florence, 1616.*

D. *Bertone di Tunis* . E. *quattro Galera che hanno albordato detto bertone*
. I. *Petaccio, che uiene in soccorso del Bertone.*

L. 195

. H. *S.ta Maria Maddalena, e s.to stefano che uanno a inuestire il Petaccio*
. I. *Galea Padrona ua a soccorrerle.* L. *Petaccio che si difende*

L. 196

8   ***Les combats de quatre galères***

Complete set of four etchings, L. 194-197, last states of two or three (**R.**), 1617.

Watermark: *Scales in a circle,* on two only.

140 x 200

Lieure says there is only one state of L. 196 but, according to a manuscript note by Osbert Barnard, there are two states:
I. *The initial* **L** *above the boat on left is in reverse.* II. *This initial is corrected (as here)*

L. 200

9   ***La Petite Place de Sienne***

L. 200, only state (**R.R.R.**), circa 1618. Nancy 227.

76 x 99

L. 278

L. 427

10   ***Le Massacre des Innocents,*** *1st plate (Florence)*

L. 278, first state of two, before the signature (**R.**), circa 1617-18. Nancy 541.

138 x 107

Sold with

Le Massacre des Innocents, *2nd plate (Nancy)*

L. 427, first state of two, before the signature (**R.**).

135 x 110

Christe tuis en pascis oues hic carnibus, ipse
et Cibus, et Pastor, moxque futurus Ouis

L. 282

11   ***La Grande Passion***

Complete set of seven etchings, circa 1619-24:

Le lavement des pieds

L. 281, second state of four. Nancy 550.

Watermark: *Interlaced 'C'* (L. 29)

109 x 214

La Cène

L. 282, first state of three. Nancy 551.

Watermark: *Interlaced 'C'* (L. 29)

112 x 217

La Condamnation à mort

L. 283, first state of two. Nancy 555.

Watermark: *Interlaced 'C'* (L. 29)

112 x 214

Le Couronnement d'épines

L. 284, second state of four. Nancy 557.

Watermark: *Huchet*

108 x 212

La Présentation au peuple

L. 285, first state of three. Nancy 561.

Watermark: *Lorraine* countermark (L. 36)

109 x 212

L. 284

Purpurea quid opus ueste? heu! num cernis ut illi
Omnia purpureo membra cruore rubent!

L. 285

Le Portement de croix

L. 286, first state of three. Nancy 564.

Watermark: *Interlaced 'C'* (L. 29)

114 x 213

Le Crucifiement

L. 287, first state of two. Nancy 566.

111 x 217

L. 288

L. 289

12   *Les trois Pantalons*

Complete set of three etchings with engraving, circa 1618-1620. These impressions, printed in France after Callot's return from Florence, all lack the lower blank borderline.

Le Pantalon, ou Cassandre

L. 288, first state of two, before the address of Silvestre. Nancy 136.

Watermark: *Lorraine* countermark (L. 35)

216 x 149

Le Capitan, ou L'Amoureux

L. 289, only state. Nancy 134.

Watermark: *Double C with cross of Lorraine* (L. 29)

217 x 148

Le Zani, ou Scapin

L. 290, only state. Nancy 135.

Watermark: *Lorraine* countermark (L. 36)

216 x 148

L. 295   L. 296

L. 297   L. 298

13   **Les quatre banquets**

Complete set of four, L. 295-8, first states of two except for L. 298 which is in the second state of three, all before the numbers.

76 x 54

14   **_L'Eventail, fête de Saint Jacques sur L'Arno_**

L. 302, second state (**R.R.**), 1619. Nancy 99.

Watermark: *Eagle in circle* (L. 20)

222 x 296 (trimmed around the extremities of the image).

L. 356

L. 358

L. 359

L. 360

---

15   ***La Grand Chasse***

L. 353, first state of four (**R.R.**), circa 1619. Nancy 400.

194 x 462

---

16   ***Les Sept Péchés capitaux***

Complete set of seven etchings, L. 354-360. L. 354 in the first state of four, before the signature (**R.R.R.**), the remainder in the first states of two, before the numbers. Nancy 678-684. *Superbia* with slight mould stains at left.

75 x 57

SERENISSIMO COSMO MAGNO QVCI ETRVRIÆ

Nundinas Impruneteanas quæ in Diui Lucæ Festo quotannis Innumerabili populi frequentia, atqs affluenti
uariarum mercium copia celebrantur, iuxta Templum insigne Nobilissima Bondelmontium Familia olim in proprio
Solo erexit/um fundatumqs ubi Deiparæ Virginis Imago, miraculorum Fœcunda, ab eodem Diuo Luca, ut fertur depicta,
ansq̃ eisuneris eruta religione summa asseruatur Colitur Jacchus Caller Nobilis Impruneteanus alienatus areq̃ incisas dedi
cauit conseuatig̃ue grati animi sui perpetuum testimonium Vin Salem DCXX

Is florentia   et excudit Nancij

L. 478

L. 510

L. 511

---

17   ***L'Impruneta***

Second version (Nancy). L. 478, first state of two, before the address of Silvestre (**R.R.**).
Nancy 236. Printed on two joined sheets of paper, the join reinforced from behind. Two parallel
vertical fold marks where folded in the album.

Watermark: *Lion with star* (L. 38)

414 x 665

18   ***Saint Livier***

L. 510, first state of two, before the signature and address of Israel, 1624. Nancy 449.

106 x 74

19   ***Frontispice de La Saincte Apocatastase***

L. 511, second state (**R.R.**), 1623. Nancy 667.

149 x 101

20   *Le Grand Rocher*

L. 512, only state (**R.**). Nancy 692. Slight areas of weak printing on the rocks, a small abrasion on the buildings in the centre. A repaired tear in the lower right corner of the blank title space.

Watermark: *Double C with cross of Lorraine* (L. 29)

196 x 276

L. 551

L. 560

21 *La Noblesse*

Complete set of twelve etchings, L. 549-560, L. 551 in the first state of two,
before the address of Silvestre, the rest only states, circa 1620-1623.
Nancy 305-316.

Approx. 144 x 92

L. 561 (detail)

22   ***La Foire de Gondreville*** *(Xeuilley)*

L. 561, first state of four, before the etched signature (**R.R.R.**). Nancy 359. With Callot's name written in manuscript in the lower left corner, the lower blank borderline trimmed.

Watermark: *Crowned cross of Lorraine*

182 x 331

L. 562

23   *Le Triomphe de la Vierge, ou Petite Thèse*

L. 562, second state of three, before the address of Silvestre. Nancy 694. Fold marks at left and bottom, where the print was folded in the album. Some mildew marks and water stains around the edges and on the verso, a few thin spots and minor tears repaired at edges, with uneven but large margins all round.

Watermark: *Countermark incorporating letter P.*

552 x 365

Etched as a frontispiece to a theological thesis for the Franciscan Friar Etienne Didelot, Rome 1625.

L. 569

L. 569, first state of three, with the text and before the damage to the lower right corner of the plate. Nancy 705. Printed on two joined sheets of paper, three horizontal fold marks where bound in the album, one reinforced with a strip of paper. Small margins at top and bottom, trimmed on or just within the platemark at the sides.

807 x 498

Etched as a frontispiece to a doctoral thesis in Physics by Prince Nicolas-François de Lorraine, Pont-à-Mousson, 1625.

L. 570   L. 571   L. 572

25 *Les sacrifices*

Complete set of three, L. 570-572, only states (**R.R.**). Nancy 686, 687, 691.

67 x 51

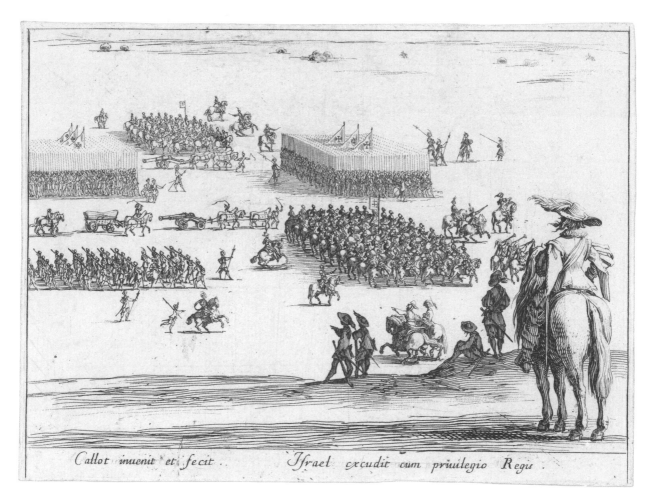

Callot inuenit et fecit .. Ifrael excudit cum priuilegio Regis .

L. 592

26 *La revue*

L. 592, first state of two (**R.R.**), circa 1628.

121 x 161

Entrée des sieurs de Vroncourt. Tyllon. et Marimont.

Callot fec.

L. 578

27   *Le Combat à la Barrière*

The complete set of 10 etchings, comprising:

Frontispiece

L. 575, second state of three. Nancy 460.

154 x 110

Entrée du Prince de Pfalzbourg

L. 576, only state. Nancy 461.

Watermark: *Lorraine* countermark (L. 36)

155 x 242

Entrée de M. de Macey

L. 577, only state. Nancy 462.

Watermark: *Lorraine* countermark (L. 36)

151 x 223

Entrée des sieurs de Vroncourt, Tyllon, et Marimont

L. 578, first state of two. Nancy 463.

Watermark: *Lorraine* countermark (L. 36)

150 x 223

Entrée de Monsieur de Couvonge et de Monsieur de Chalabre

L. 579, only state. Nancy 466.

Watermark: *Angel* (L. 26/27)

154 x 243

Entrée de Monsieur le Comte de Brionne

L. 580, only state. Nancy 468.

Watermark: *Angel* (L. 26/27)

154 x 243

Entrée de Monsieur Henry de Lorraine

L. 581, only state. Nancy 471.

Watermark: *Lorraine* countermark (L. 36)

154 x 242

Entrée de son Altesse représentant le Soleil

L. 582, only state. Nancy 473.

Watermark: *Angel* (L. 26/27)

154 x 242

Entrée de son Altesse à pied

L. 583, second state. Nancy 474.

Watermark: *Angel* (L. 26/27)

153 x 242

Combat à la Barrière

L. 584, only state. Nancy 475.

Watermark: *Angel* (L. 26/27)

152 x 239

Combat à la Barrière *records a festival in honour of the Duchesse de Chevreuse, Nancy, 1627. The complete set of ten prints listed above were published in a book with explanatory text by Henry Humbert. The etchings were vertically folded in that edition. Our impressions are exceptionally fine and have no fold marks.*

Sold with:
A. Entrée de Mons. de Couvonge et de Mons. de Chalabre

L. 585, only state (**R.**). Nancy 467.

75 x 232

B. Entrée de Monseigneur Henry de Lorraine

L. 586, first state of four, the print cut in six sections but from one plate, in the second state the plate itself was cut in six. (**R.R.R.R.**). Nancy 472.

Watermark: *Bunch of grapes*

Each approx. 73 x 120

These alternative plates are variants of two subjects from the series, of different size, and were not included in the published edition.

Cet entrée est de Monsieur le Comte
de Brionne Grand Chambelan de
son Altesse, representant Jason

Callot fec.

Entrée de son Altesse a pied

Jac. Callot In. et fecit

TABVLA
OBSIDIONIS
BREDANAE.

L. 593, the complete set of six etchings, together with three sheets of explanation, and the printed title. Nancy 479-480.

The six main sections in the only recorded states apart from the *lower right section,* which is in the first state of two, before the address of Silvestre and the *top centre section,* also in the first state of two, before the inscription **Siège de Breda.**

Watermark: *Small posthorn*

Each section 690 x 461

Tables of Description

Three sheets with four columns of text on each, the last with the publication line
ANTVERPIAE, TYPIS PLANTINIANIS, M. DC. XXVIII.

Title

Printed in three lines on one sheet, intended to be cut and assembled as a title at the top of the plan.

R.R.R.R. *The incredibly rare first state of this major etching, printed on uncut sheets, with irregular margins. Horizontal fold marks where folded in the album, some mould stains on versos. The sheets have never been joined and are sold as they are.*

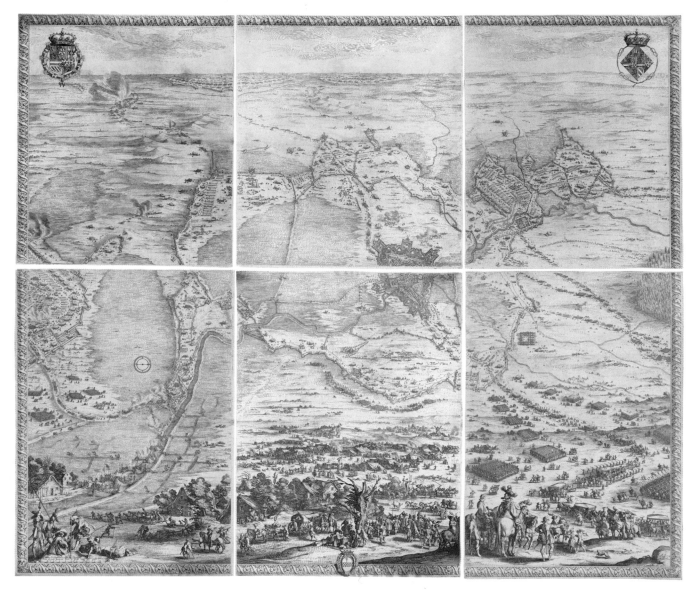

L. 593

L. 594

---

29   **Les martyrs de Japon**

L. 594, first state of two. Nancy 632.

Watermark: *countermark of letters,* similar to L. 41.

168 x 112

Etched circa 1627 when the Crucified Missionaries were Beatified by Pope Urban VIII.

---

30   **Le débarquement des troupes**

L. 653, first state of three, with the address of Israel, circa 1627. Nancy 489.
With a > shaped tear repaired centre right, visible on the verso.

138 x 384

Probably intended as a border decoration to the Siège de l'Ile de Ré, *but not published as such.*

Callot fecit.

Israel excudit.

L. 654 (detail)

31   *Le Siège de la Citadelle de St-Martin, dans l'Ile de Ré*

L. 654, 656-659, 1627. The complete set of six etchings, together with the ornamental surrounding border. Nancy 485.

L. 654, the six main sections, all in the second or third states of two or three, with the initial letters in the upper corners.

Watermark: *Three fleur de lys in crowned shield*

Each section 575 x 435

L. 656-9, the top and bottom borders, in six sections, in the second states of two, or three (**R.**).

The side borders, in four sections, in the only states (**R.R.**).

Only the six central sections are by Callot. The ornamental borders are the work of Michel Lasne, Abraham Bosse and, perhaps, Charles Delorme. The main sections are with irregular margins, with horizontal fold marks where folded in the album. The lower centre section has a short paper split repaired, some mould marks on the versos and slight water stains at the edges of the margins. The borders have some crease and fold marks where bound in the album. The sheets have never been joined and are sold as they are.

L. 655 (detail)

32   *Le Siège de la Rochelle*

L. 655, 660-1, 1628. The complete set of six etchings, together with the ornamental surrounding border. Nancy 490.

L. 655, the six main sections, all in the second states of two.

Watermark: *Three fleur de lys in crowned shield*

Each section 564 x 449

L. 660-661, the top and bottom borders, in six sections, varying states but all with the registration initials except for the lower right section which is before that letter, (**R.**).

The side borders, in four sections, in the only states (**R.R.**).

As with the Siège de l'Ile de Ré *only the central section is by Callot. The ornamental borders are the work of Michel Lasne, Abraham Bosse and Israel Henriet. The prints are in similar condition to the previous item.*

L. 662

33   **Portrait de Charles Delorme**

L. 662, second state (**R.R.**), 1630. Nancy 693.

Watermark: Indistinct *Huchet in shield*, see L. 44-49.

187 x 115

Using the clarification of states listed by M. Hubert Prouté our impression has all the characteristics of the second state apart from detail 5, which corresponds to the first state.

34   **Combat d'Avigliano**

L. 663, first state of two (**R.R.R.**), 1630. Nancy 491. With a vertical fold mark where bound in the album, and a slight printing crease lower right centre, very large margins.

352 x 530

SCEPTRIS FAMA
SVPERBVM EVEHIT

LVDOVICO DECIMO TERTIO IVSTO. PIO. FELICI. AVGVSTO. INVICTO. MAGNO. TRIVMPHATORI. ITALICO.
BRITANNICO. ALEMANNICO. LOTHARINGICO. FRANCIAE ET NAVARRAE REGI CHRISTIANISSIMO.
ÆTATIS SVÆ ANNO 33. ET SVI REGNI 23.

Iussu Regis Christianissimi Michael Asinius sculptor regius sculpsit regisq. cælestis auree domini millesimo sexcentesimo trigesimo quarto huius tabulæ ab As. inu. et cæs. exempl. vendenda prostant in sua domo sub reg peristilio.   *Cum privilegio Regis Christ.*

L. 664

forty six

L. 666

35   **Portrait de Louis XIII**

Engraving by Michel Lasne, the etched background by Callot, L. 664, second state (**R.R.**), circa 1630 (published 1634). With a horizontal fold mark where bound in the album, some printing creases across the background and the front hooves of the rearing horse. A tear repaired at the upper right, some mould marks on the verso, with margins.

624 x 435

The landscape background by Callot is similar, but in reverse, to that of the Combat d'Avigliano *(see previous entry).*

36   **Frontispice de la Sacra Cosmologia**

L. 666, second state, 1630 (?). Nancy 706.

139 x 94

L. 667

37   **Vue du Louvre**

L. 667, second state of five, 1629. Nancy 436.
With a very large margin at the top and small margins on the other three sides.

Watermark: *Interlaced 'C' with lion with star* (L. 29 and L. 38/9)

167 x 336

38   **Vue du Pont-Neuf**

L. 668, first state of five, before the signature (**R.R.R.R.**), 1629. Nancy 438.
With large margins at the top and bottom and small margins at the side.

Watermark: *Interlaced 'C' with lion with star* (L.29 and L. 38/9)

136 x 337

L. 677

L. 678

39   **L'Assomption**

L. 677, first state of three, before the signature and inscription on the tomb (**R.**). Nancy 591.

90 x 68

40   **Jésus en Croix**

Outline etching, L. 678, second state.

86 x 66

41   **Portrait de Claude Deruet**

L. 1296, second state of five (**R.R.R.**), 1632. Nancy 459.
A few mould spots on verso, two showing on recto to the right of the sitter's head.

298 x 171

Ce fameux Createur de tant de beaux visages
S'estoit assez tiré dans ses rares Ouurages
Où la Nature et L'art admirent leurs efforts
Il tenoit le desseus du Temps et de L'enuie
Et luy de quy les mains ressuscitent les Morts
Pouuoit bien par soy mesme eterniser sa vie

Mais quand Il eust fallu laisser quelque autre marque
Qui malgré les rigueurs du Sort et de la Parque
Le monstrast tout entier a la Posterité
Son huile et ses Couleurs pour le faire reuiure
Au goust des mieux sensez auroient tousiours esté
Vn Charme plus puissant q̃ l'eau fort et le Cuiure

A Claude Deruet Escuier Cheualier de l'ordre de Portugal Son fidele Amy Iacques Callot F

L. 1304

Les Grands Apôtres

Complete set of sixteen etchings, L. 1297-1312, the title in the only state, the rest in the second states of three, before the numbers, except for L. 1304 and 1310 which are in the first states of three (**R.R.R.**), 1631. Nancy 597-600 (four exhibited).

145 x 96

Callot fec.

L. 1310

L. 1313

L. 1314

43   *Les combats de cavalerie*

Pair of etchings, L. 1313-1314, first states of two, before the numbers, circa 1633. Nancy 496-497.

46 x 94

L. 1333

L. 1335

L. 1336

Les petites Misères de la Guerre

Complete set of title (by Abraham Bosse), and six etchings, L. 1333-1338, second states, circa 1632 (published 1636). Nancy 501-506.

57 x 117

L. 1371   L. 1363

L. 1366   L. 1368

45   **_La Vie de la St Vierge_**

Complete set of fourteen etchings, L. 1357-1370, L. 1357 in the second state of two, the remainder in the second states of three, with letters but before numbers. Nancy 587-589 (three exhibited).

71 x 45

Sold with

L'Annonciation

L. 1371, second state (**R.R.**).

65 x 45

The very rare supernumerary plate.

L. 1386   L. 1390

L. 1395   L. 1400

46   *Les petits Apôtres*

Complete set of sixteen etchings, L. 1386-1401, the title in the second state of three (**R.R.R.**), the remainder in the first states of four (**R.R.R.**), all before the address of Israel, 1632. Nancy 638-653.

72 x 45

Supplicium Sceleri Frænum

Voy, lécteur, comme la Justice   Pour le repos de L'uniuers,   Par l'aspect de ceste figure   Pour heureusement t'exempter
Par tant de Supplices diuers,   Punir des Meschans la malice,   Tu dois tous crimes euiter,   Des effectz de la forfaicture.

L. 1402

Ce partement soudain sert comme de presage,
Que le calme trop grand est suivy de l'orage.
Cum priuilege Reg. Israel excu

L. 1406

Dans les charmes du vin et de la volupté
Ce prodigue se perd en sa brutalité.
Cum priuilege Reg. Israel excudit

L. 1407

Celuy qui dédaignoit les plus friands morceaux.
Se va nourrir de glands destinez aux porceaux:
Cum priuilege Reg. Israel excu

L. 1409

Afligé de le voir de misere transy.
Ce bon Vieillard l'embrasse et le prend à mercy.
Cum priuilege Reg. Israel excudit

L. 1411

---

47   ***Les supplices***

L. 1402, second state of eight, with only two windows in the square tower in the background
(**R.R.**). Nancy 528.

Watermark: *Huchet*

112 x 216

48   ***La Vie de L'Enfant Prodigue***

Complete set of eleven etchings, L. 1404-1414, the title in the second state of two, the rest in the
second states of three, before the numbers, 1635. Nancy 348-358.

60 x 80

L. 1415

L. 1415, only state.

76 x 93

(L. 188.) Printed from two plates, joined down the centre. Horizontal and vertical creases where folded in the album, some strengthened on the verso. The verso with some water stains, not visible on recto.

Watermark: *Fleur de lys in a circle surmounted by the initial M* (right sheet); *Figure in shield,* for the type see Heawood 1351, Briquet 7628 (left sheet).

745 x 930

Although the album from which these prints came contained a few rather unusual rarities it did not include the original of the impossibly rare 1ère version of La Tentation de St Antoine, *Florence, c. 1617 (the plate was spoiled after only a few impressions had been taken). It did however contain this enlarged copy in reverse, signed Antonius Mei Tinghius and dated 1637. This is mentioned in a footnote to L. 188, and the Coburg impression is described and illustrated in Hollstein,* German series XXV, p. 34, No. 1, *where it is given to Anton Meitingh. The five prints listed there are all Florentine productions.*

SER. FERDINANDO II. HEIRVRIE MAG. DVCI V E MAGNO INGENIORVM MECOENATI. INSIGNEM. D. ANTONII DE... ... IBERRIMO VICTORIAM SVA MANV. INCISAM. ET IMPRESSAM ANTONIVS MEI [INGHI-RAT. DONAE. DICAT. CDI.XXXVI]

ILLVSTRISSIMO MAXIMOQVE VIRO D.D. LVDOVICO PHELYPEAVX DÑO.
DE LAVRILIERE, COMITI CONSISTORLINO SACRARVM IVSSIONVM VIRO
DEDICAT CONSECRATQVE.
IA. CALLOT VOVET

Informes lacrua. caccis frabulata latebris
Monfra fuum rupere Chaos, atque agmine facto
Lætifera orbem violant lucemque venenis.
Sit scelerum facies Erebo mutavit Erinnum.
Interea vefti quid agas fub fervice facri

Sunote fonces tantos fentis et despicis hoftes!
Nil fperat mortale tibi nec faudia pectus.
Blanda manent, nec frangit Amor, nec fanem terrant.
Illæ rufticæ polo reparatas quæ ad Origine vires
Infinnet in terris quas videt in æther pugnas

Cam. Privil. Reg.   Ifrael excu 1635

La derniere planche grauée par deffunt Callot, a laquelle l'eau forte n'a esté donnée .quapres sa mort-

L. 1428

---

51   **La Tentation de St Antoine,** *deuxième planche*

L. 1416, second state of five, before the alteration to the coat of arms and the addition of
IIII in the text between *Iussionum* and *Viro* (**R.R.R.R.**), 1635. Nancy 536 (an impression of the
third state).

Watermark: *large bunch of grapes*

354 x 460

*An exceptionally rare early impression, trimmed to the borderline and with a vertical crease mark
where bound in the album. Some mould spots and thinned areas of paper on the verso.*

---

52   **La petite treille**

L. 1428, second state of three (**R.R.R.**). Nancy 715.

80 x 163

With the famous inscription in the title space La derniere planche gravée par deffunt Callot, a
laquelle l'eau-forte n'a esté donnée quapres sa mort.